To be effective, the yoga postures (asanas) described and illustrated in Shrihat Satva Yoga require musical elixirs, free with purchase of the book. To obtain your copy of this music, two options are offered:

A. To download the music, go to www.yogaofillumination.com;

B. To obtain the physical CDs, you may either:

    a. email spiritualjourneys_hilda@yahoo.com, providing your name and mailing address, or

    b. call toll-free 877 552-5646 or 502 499 0016.

The effectiveness of this modality is heightened by at least 15 minutes of meditation on a verse from The Poetry of Dreaming, accompanied by music from the elixirs, prior to beginning the yoga.

SHRIHAT SATVA YOGA

The Yoga to Clear Past Incarnations

Almine

Practical Wisdom for Spiritual Mastery

Published by Spiritual Journeys LLC

Copyright 2010 MAB 998 Megatrust

By Almine
Spiritual Journeys LLC
P.O. Box 300
Newport, Oregon 97365

All rights reserved. No part of this publication may be reproduced without crediting Almine as the author and originator of this material.

Cover Layout by Rogier Chardet

Cover Art by Dorian Dyer
Website: www.visionheartart.com

Interior design and layout by Ariel Frailich

www.spiritualjourneys.com
Toll-free number 877 552-5646

Manufactured in the United States of America

ISBN (Softcover)
ISBN 978-1-934070-16-1 (Adobe Reader)

Contents

Endorsements V
About the Author VII

Introduction to Shrihat Satva Yoga
Introduction 3

The Poetry of Dreaming
24 Verses for Meditation 9
The 24 Verses 11
The Scroll of Namud 19

How to do the Yoga
Method 23
The 12 Postures of the Most Recent Incarnational Cycles 25
The 12 Postures of the Oldest Incarnation Cycles 43
Closing 59
Epilogue 61

Appendix I 65
Appendix II 67

Endorsements

"What a priceless experience to be able to catch a glimpse into one of the most remarkable lives of our time…"
—H.E. Ambassador Armen Sarkissian,
Former Prime Minister of the Republic of Armenia,
Astro-physicist, Cambridge University, U.K.

"I'm really impressed with Almine and the integrity of her revelations. My respect for her is immense and I hope that others will find as much value in her teaching as I have."
—Dr. Fred Bell, Former NASA Scientist

"The information she delivers to humanity is of the highest clarity. She is fully deserving of her reputation as the leading mystic of our age."
—Zbigniew Ostas, Ph.D. Quantum Medicine,
Somatidian Orthobiology, Canada and Poland

About the Author

Almine is a mystic, healer and teacher who traveled for years through many countries, empowering thousands of individuals who were drawn to her comprehensible delivery of advanced metaphysical concepts. In the wake of her humility and selfless service, unspeakable miracles have followed.

In her life, made rich by the mystical and the holy, she has stood face-to-face with many of the ancient Masters of light, retaining full memory of the ancient holy languages in both written and spoken form.

Her teachings are centered on the idea that it is not only possible to live a life of mastery and love, but that it is the birthright of every human to attain such levels of perfection. Her journey has become one of learning to live in the physical, maintaining the delicate balance of remaining self-aware while being fully expanded.

"When we live in the moment, we live in the place of power, aligned with eternal time and the intent of the Infinite. Our will becomes blended with that of the Divine."
—Almine

Introduction to Shrihat Satva Yoga

CLEARING PAST INCARNATIONAL CYCLES

The dolphin jumps through the hoop of the moon.
Rings ripple through the stars.

Introduction

Cosmic cycles of life fall into two categories: those that can be called the ascension cycles and those that are called the descension cycles.

There are 12 electrical, masculine, light-based cycles; these are the ascension cycles. Likewise there are 12 cycles of a feminine, magnetic, frequency-based nature. Each of these has been repeated many times by all creatures as incarnation cycles.

The unresolved issues of those cycles, such as old belief systems, memories of pain and other distorted emotions are presented for resolution in dreams. There are 24 depths of dreaming, with the 12 more shallow ones communicating to us through dream symbols. The 12 deepest dream states are the feminine, non-cognitive states that cannot be interpreted through dream symbols and produce what to us seems like a deep, dreamless sleep. They speak to us through art and the Poetry of Dreaming.

This unique poetry communicates through omissions – that which is not said – imparting multiple depths of meaning revealing themselves as feelings and qualities. Although the Poetry of Dreaming uses literary devices such as assonance, alliteration, personification and sustained epithets, their use has profound purpose that transcends the obvious. The same applies to the use of adjectives in this type of poetry.

Its concise but powerful descriptive quality is reminiscent of the poetic form called Haiku, but whereas Haiku is bound by a rigid structure, the Poetry of Dreaming is not. Haiku provides the essence of simplicity that lies within the complexity of appearances. The Poetry of Dreaming whispers, through its rich imagery, of the primordial origins of the moment.

THE ROLE OF SHRIHAT SATVA YOGA IN ATTAINING ENLIGHTENMENT

Upon reaching a high level of enlightenment, the master becomes an androgynous being. Having lost all other identities, he or she now loses the identity of gender. This is done by balancing the proactive and receptive qualities within. Resolving the 12 feminine and 12 masculine incarnation cycles brings this desired state to fruition.

In the practice of Shrihat Satva Yoga, multiple elements are combined to facilitate the removal of debris from previous incarnations.

- The musical elixirs used are an exact balance of black (subliminal) and white frequencies, utilizing the alchemical potencies of frequencies to balance out illusion. They form an essential component of this yoga practice.
- The Poetry of Dreaming is used to open non-cognitive communication with the deeper states of dreaming. This allows the issues of very old cycles of life to come to the surface for cancellation by the sound elixirs.
- The breathing rhythms and eye movement patterns of an individual reveal retained and suppressed trauma. Shrihat Satva Yoga uses these to trigger the release of debris from old incarnations.
- Shrihat Satva Yoga's postures frequently have the limbs crossing over one another. This is to facilitate merging the masculine and feminine into the androgyny of enlightenment. They are also designed to open the gates of dreaming in the body.[1]

The human body is unique in that it is an exact microcosm of the macrocosm of created life. There are 12 points along the right, mas-

---

1 This form of yoga could be very beneficial for certain ADD and other behavioral disorders in children

culine side of the body and the same number on the left side. These are microcosmic replicas of the macrocosmic cycles of life.

The yoga postures are designed to open and remove the debris from these points – the gates of dreaming. This will occur physically through the postures and the music. Dissolving debris also occurs by way of dreaming (triggered by the breathing and eye movements), releasing past issues that caused the blockages in the points.

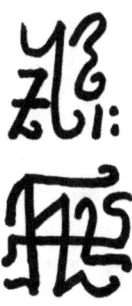

The Poetry of Dreaming

THE MEDITATION TO PREPARE FOR THE YOGA

Where earth and sky merge in horizonless white,
a circle of muskoxen stand alone together.

24 Verses for Meditation

FOR THE TEACHER

NOTE: Before beginning the yoga, each student should read Disclaimer of Liability found in the Appendix. Teachers should retain copies in their files.

It is recommended that only a single verse be meditated on during a ten to fifteen minute period preparatory to commencing the yoga session. Have the meditation music playing and invite students to arrive 15 minutes before class to prepare themselves, entering the room quietly and meditating.

The music for this purpose is unique and irreplaceable for the purpose because it is sung in the solfeggio scale. This is the scale used for Gregorian chants until it was banned by the Catholic Church in the early Middle Ages. Its effect of liberating the listener from belief systems is profound.

The yoga instructor should have the chosen verse accessible, either displayed in large letters or as a handout for the students as they enter and remove their shoes.

The method is simple. The student reads the verse, empties his or her mind through entering a meditative state, and simply observes any images that arise and the subtle feelings they evoke.

During longer meditations this process should be done no more than three times in an hour[2]. The student needs at least 10 minutes to rest and integrate the new qualities he or she feels within.

---

2 Using three different verses for an hour meditation.

At no time should analysis be used. The more empty the mind, the more successful the non-cognitive communication from the deep psyche can be. Capturing in writing the images that arise can be helpful. Students should not think they have failed if in 15 minutes only a word is received. Different students may receive communications in different forms.

Note: A special class could be given on the verses. The initial verse is like the end of a thread that is followed into the labyrinth of the deep chambers of the psyche. The images that arise from each 15-minute meditation are written down.

The 24 Verses

The desert wind sings to the serpents' undulating dance
in the sand. Heat waves join in the merriment.

The fanciful flight of a blue butterfly, the insistent hum of a bee.
Sun-warmed berries like gems strung on the mulberry tree.

The yellow moon watches the canoe split the chilly silence of
the lake. The sound of paddles floats on the breath of the night.

The Poetry of Dreaming

Snow geese fly through puffy skies. Snow-engorged
pines wait on the mountain below.

Where earth and sky merge in horizonless white,
a circle of muskoxen stand alone together.

In the day's last rays a dragonfly plays.
A robin sings its way to the nest.

The 24 Verses

The dolphin jumps through the hoop of the moon. Rings ripple through the stars.

Wild geese like a clanging chain pull the moon from the web of the willow tree.

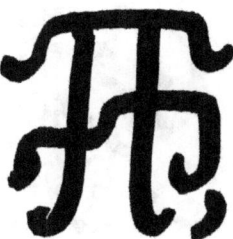

The corn fields, like weary battle grounds after the harvest, wait with abated breath as the world turns through the last rays of summer.

The Poetry of Dreaming

In utter silence the frozen lake lies. Northern lights reach with greedy fingers to catch a falling star.

In dizzy heights, eagles clasped in a mating embrace of tumbled passion fall to earth. A downy feather floats upon the wind.

The nightingale rolls his notes like silver beads across the dome of the night, dropping them into the wishing well.

The 24 Verses

With lusty gusto the yellow dandelion reaches its head
above the manicured lawn to embrace the sun.

Dew on the dunes where dark footsteps lie and a
seagull in mourning that turns through the sky.

Four white doves, light as sighs, turn as one through the
arc of the sky. Their shadows like crows follow below.

The Poetry of Dreaming

A flock of grey doves hang like a bunch of grapes from the trellis of the sky. The monastery bells call them home.

Cumulus formations like Spanish galleons adrift in an endless sky, jostling one another to see the spring lambs birthed.

Daffodils prance and preen as they are teased by the mischievous midday breeze. A dappled fawn sleeps in the yellow meadow.

The endless song of crickets in the dune grass, the rhythmic breaths of the sea, lull drowsy seagulls into a hypnotic sleep.

Where shimmering grey skies and ocean meet, a little white boat lies adrift like a pearl in an oyster.

The red berries of the holly tree – a startling surprise to the North Wind inspecting his snow-clad domain.

The Poetry of Dreaming

Above stony crags where eagles fly, mighty wings ride the winds. A piercing cry that splits the sky echoes across the valley from side to side.

On mesa heights under pregnant skies, nostrils flare and wild horses swallow the wind.

Captured inside the rain puddle lies the cloudy sky – the infinite within the finite confined.

The Scroll of Namud

(EXCERPT)

TRANSLATION OF THE SCROLL OF NAMUD

From the Motherland[3] we call Shalmali, great wisdom was spread to the peoples of the Earth. Wise masters called Nagas[4], which means 'gates of wisdom', were sent to teach. They took tablets of knowledge with them and separated into groups of two, copying these tablets so that they could share them with different people.

They taught the Naga language to all in walled temples called 'Chaldi'[5] or 'Kaldi', meaning 'walls'. Seven sets of holy records were taken through high mountains (Himalayas) to the land of Monassa (India) and placed in Kaldi temples in seven cities. The records were kept by divinely inspired poets or sages called 'Rishis' and these seven cities became known as Rishi cities.

The records taught yoga, which means 'gates of the body' to the people. The greatest of these was Devi Satva Yoga.

Devi Satva Yoga was designed to create enlightenment by opening three sets of gates in the human body; three bodies of Yoga were used for this – Irash Satva Yoga, Shrihat Satva Yoga and Saradesi Satva Yoga.

Minikva ares prihat uruva hachte.
Within man are the answers to the starry skies.

---

3 Lumeria.
4 Called Naguals or Nacaals in some tongues.
5 Where the Biblical nation, the Chaldeans, get their name.

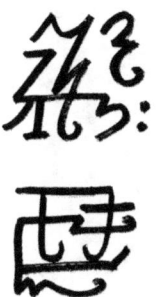

How to do the Yoga

Wild geese, like a clanging chain, pull the moon
from the web of the willow tree.

Method

There are 24 yoga postures that correspond to the 24 accompanying sound elixirs. Each posture is held during the entire duration of its corresponding sound elixir.

Gradually ease into the posture if you are not athletically active. If dizzy at any time, lie flat on your back. At no time should you do more than a gentle, comfortable stretch. You should be comfortably warm to stimulate the release of toxins. A pillow may be used for support as needed until flexibility is restored. The use of a yoga mat is recommended.

The yoga may be taught to others if the practitioner has become proficient in its practices. No other training is needed because its effectiveness is inherent in its components.[6]

---

6   See important notes regarding use of the material in the Appendix.

The 12 Postures of the Most Recent Incarnational Cycles

Mish tanarech urastu minavit hereshta subit,
kanesh piresa unesta haruvit

If life is a dream, let me be a lucid dreamer
until I can fully awaken

THE 12 MASCULINE POSTURES – KLANISH HUBAVI

These postures release the debris of the 12 most recent cycles of incarnation cycles, speaking to us in symbols through the 12 most shallow dream cycles[7].

1. **Posture No. 1 – Klinaveshvi**
   - Sit comfortably with your legs crossed, back straight and shoulders relaxed.
   - Reach both arms straight out in front of you, palms facing outwards.
   - Cross your arms over each other while keeping them straight.
   - Clasp your palms together.
   - Bend your elbows and bring your clasped hands down, under and up onto your chest.
   - Take a deep breath and exhale in a long sigh while dropping the chin down onto your chest and closing your eyes.
   - Keep your back straight and continue the breaths.
   - Hold the posture for the duration of the sound elixir.

   This clears the corpus callosum in the midbrain of communication blockages between the masculine and feminine.

---

7 The Labyrinth of the Moon will contain 144 additional verses of Poetry of Dreaming and multiple dream symbols for interpreting the shallow dream state.

How to do the Yoga

Posture No. 1

2. Posture No. 2 – Nek-varavi-esva

- Holding the same posture as in No. 1, raise your head upward while rolling your eyes upward.
- Slowly lower your head to your chest, rolling your eyes downward.
- Breathe in when the head goes up, sigh the breath out when the head moves down.
- Repeat head and eye movements for the duration of the sound elixir.

This clears the feelings held in the astral body.

How to do the Yoga

3. **Posture No. 3 – Nek-bilaveshvi**
   - Using the same body posture as in No. 2, move the head left while rolling the eyes left and breathing in. The chin must stay level.
   - Breathe out while moving the head and eyes right.
   - The relaxed shoulders remain facing to the front.
   - Repeat for the duration of the sound elixir.

   This clears memories of auditory input that cause reactionary responses to audio stimuli.

4. Posture No. 4 – Nek-savasutvi

- In the same position as in the previous two postures, roll the head as follows:
- Start with the chin down on your chest, eyes looking down.
- While drawing your breath in, keep your chin straight and roll your head up and to the left until you are looking left. The eyes move from straight down to where eleven o'clock would be. In other words, your eyes will be looking half way between the crown of your head and your left ear.

How to do the Yoga

- While blowing your breath out, move your head in an arc to a level position on the right, rolling your eyes down and up to between the crown of your head and your right ear.
- Repeat.

This clears visionary memories from the eyes and optical nerves to remove obsolete debris that still impact our responses to visual stimuli.

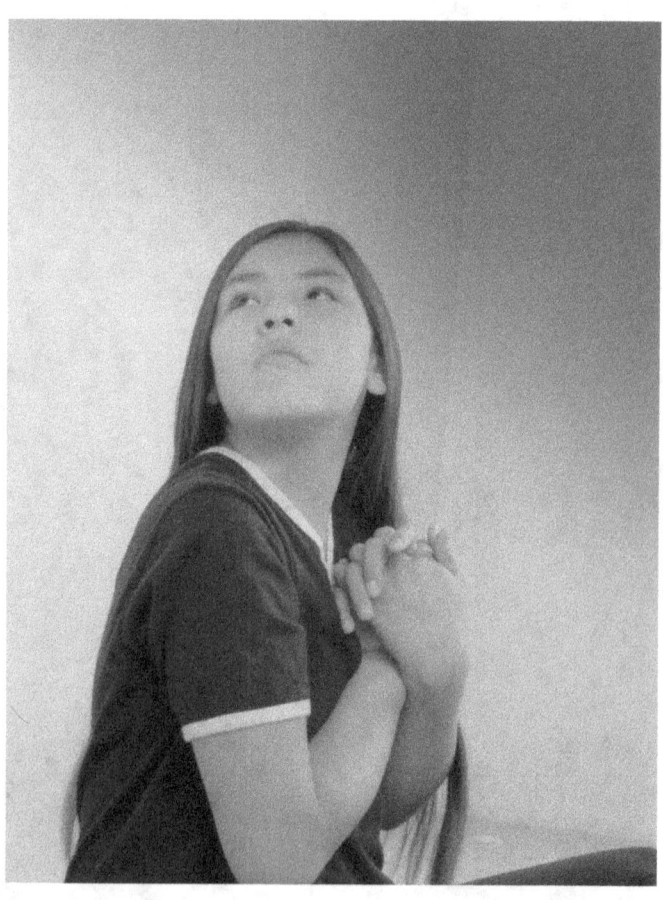

5. Posture No. 5 – Sihiravat-nesvi

- While sitting, bend your knees and cross your ankles, creating a slightly opened cross-legged position. The feet will be slightly extended in front of you, legs relaxed. Brace the knees with pillows if you need support.
- Crossing the arms over one another, hold the ball of the left foot with the left hand and the ball of the right foot with the right hand.
- With back straight, lean forward into a comfortable stretch and lower your head onto your chest.

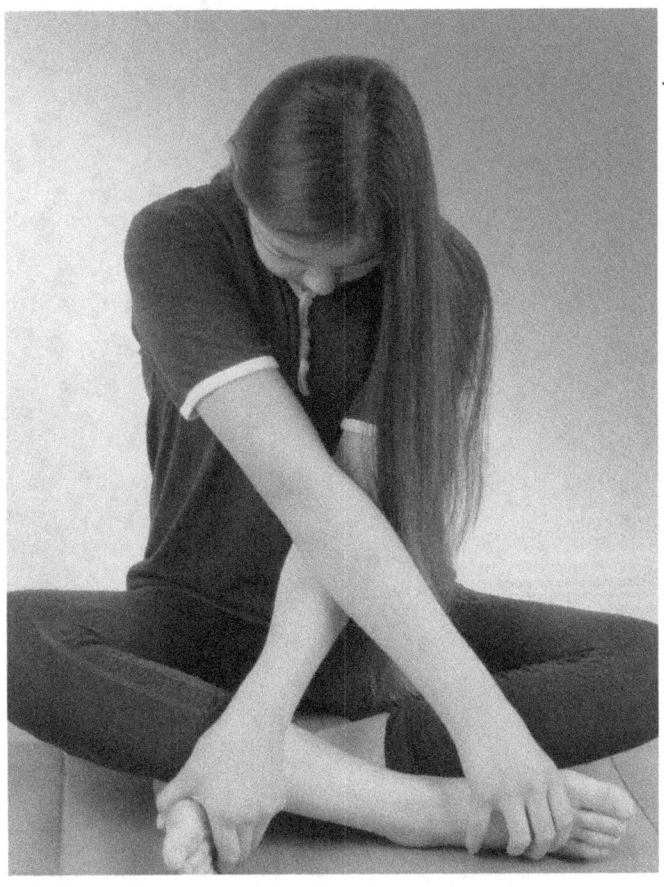

How to do the Yoga

- With eyes closed, roll them down as far as they will go. This clears feelings of being unsupported and insecure.

Note: If you push with your thumbs into the middle of the foot just below the ball of the foot, it will facilitate the benefits of this posture.

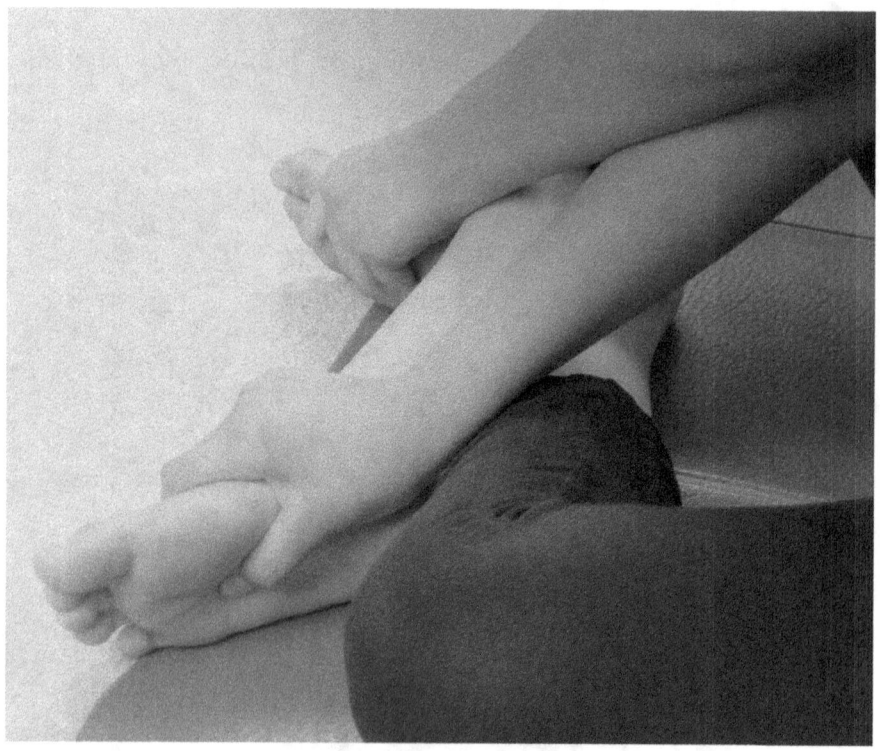

6. Posture No. 6 – **Nichtane-survat**
- Remain in the same leg position as in No. 5 but raise the knees without moving the feet. The knees move from an outward, spread position toward the center.
- Reach the arms around the outside of the knees and grasp the ball of the left foot with the right hand and the ball of the right foot with the left hand.
- Relax the knees inside the cradle of the arms.
- With spine straight, raise the chin and tilt the head backward to look up as far as it will comfortably go.

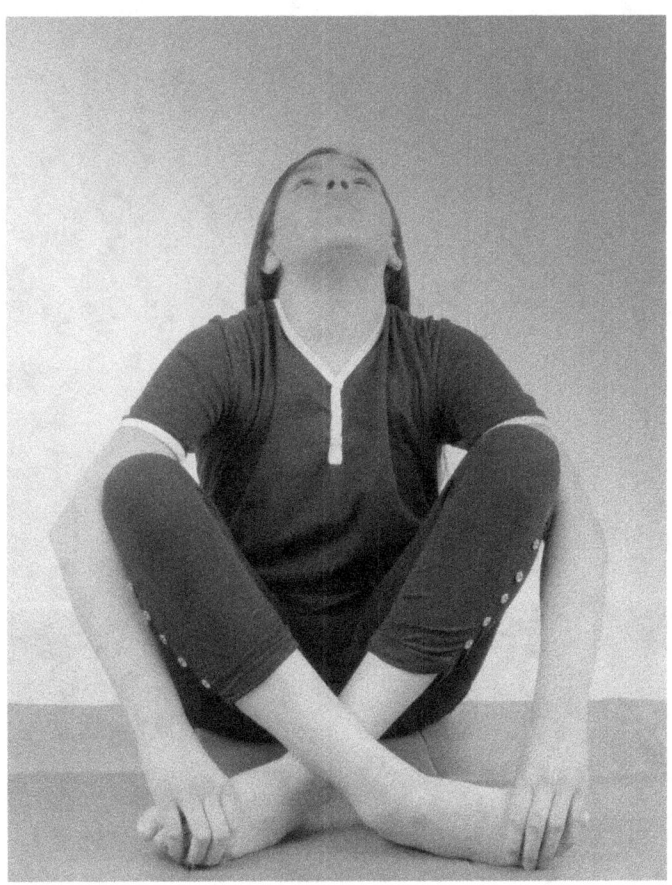

How to do the Yoga

- Roll the open eyes upward.

This releases attachment to obsolete standards of excellence and promotes genius, which is effortless knowing.

Note: If you push with your thumb in the middle of the top of the ball of the foot directly below the space between your 2nd and 3rd toes, it will facilitate increase of the benefits of this posture.

7. **Posture No. 7 – Kinavesh-uvasu**
   - With knees relaxed to the outside (brace them with pillows if you need to), place the soles of the feet together.

The 12 Postures of the Most Recent Incarnational Cycles

- With arms extended straight in front of you and your back straight, lean forward clasping your left foot in your left hand and your right foot in your right hand.
- Press with your thumbs approximately 2" below the base of your big toe, right below the ball of the foot.
- Turn your head to the right and with your chin on your right shoulder, roll your eyes around in a clockwise circle for the duration of the accompanying sound elixir.
- If your neck feels strained or you feel dizzy, drop your head onto your chest and close your eyes.

This posture promotes the dissolving of the matrices of space and directions. Mastery is to live in spaceless space.

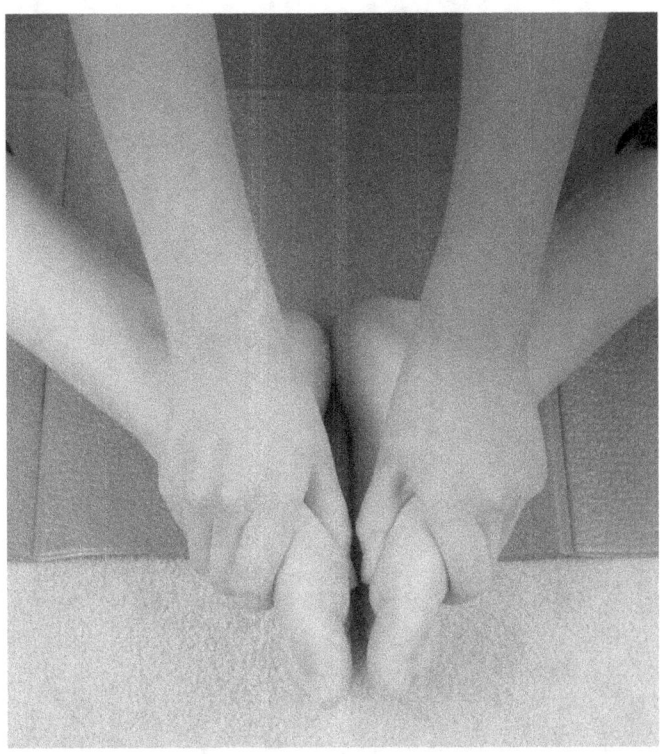

How to do the Yoga

8. **Posture No. 8 – Usatrech-uvasu**
   - With knees relaxed to the outside (brace them with pillows if you need to), place the soles of the feet together.
   - With arms extended straight in front of you and your back straight, lean forward clasping your left foot in your left hand and your right foot in your right hand.
   - Press with your thumbs approximately 2" below the base of your big toe, right below the ball of the foot.
   - Turn your head to the left and with your chin on your left shoulder, roll your eyes around in a counter-clockwise circle for the duration of the accompanying sound elixir.

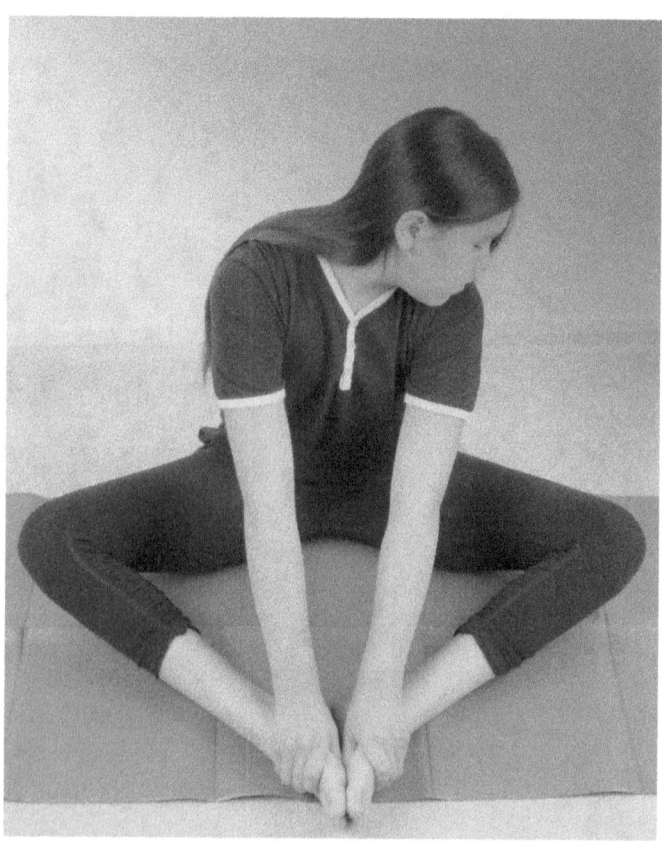

- If your neck feels strained or you feel dizzy, drop your head onto your chest and close your eyes.

This posture promotes the dissolving of the matrices of linear time. Mastery is to live in timelessness.

9. **Posture No. 9 – Perivat-huraveshvi**
   - Lie flat on your back with your legs straight.
   - Keeping them together, bend your knees until, with outstretched arms, you can grasp and support your knees.
   - Cross your feet.
   - Close your eyes, and with the tip of your tongue push into the middle of the hard palate for the duration of the sound elixir.
   - Deepen the in-breath, sigh it out.

This assists in healing addictions and memory patterns that create cravings.

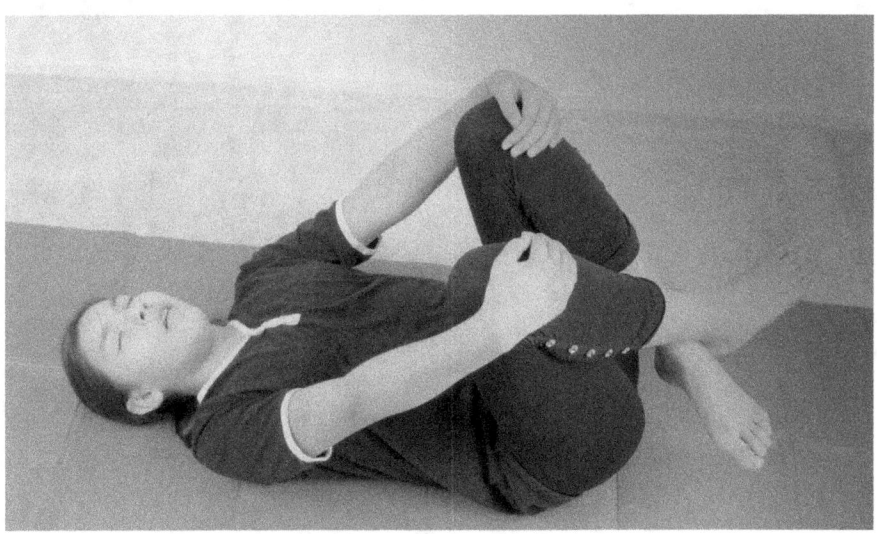

How to do the Yoga

10. Posture No. 10 – Nichstave-huraveshvi
- Lie flat on your back with your left leg straight and your right knee bent. The knee is pointing straight up at the ceiling.
- Place your left heel (the area of the lower Achilles tendon) on top of the right knee in a comfortable position.
- Move the left knee out to the side.
- Place your palms together with your arms resting comfortably on your chest.
- Push your fingertips gently but firmly against the tip of your chin.
- Breathe deeply in the same way as in Posture 9.

The purpose of this posture is described below in Posture 11.

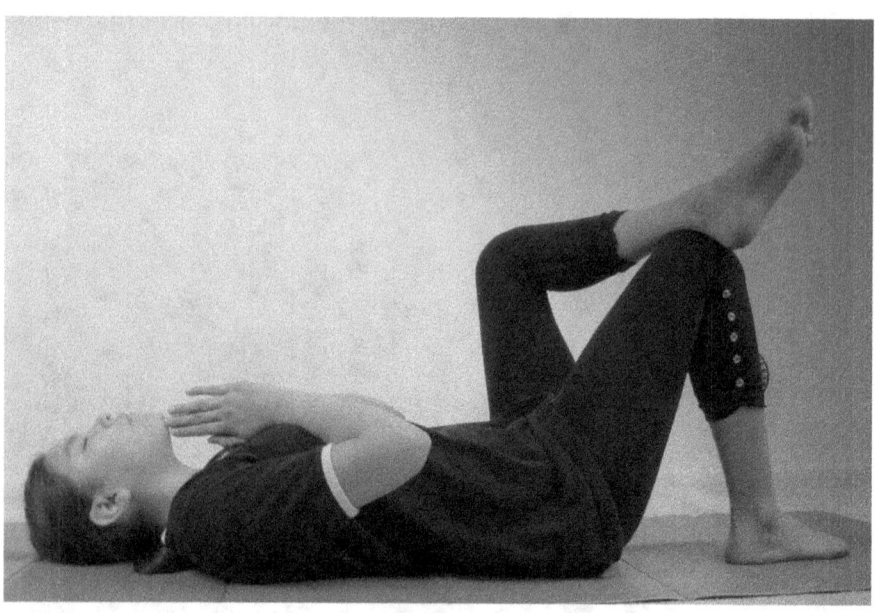

The 12 Postures of the Most Recent Incarnational Cycles

11. Posture No. 11 – Kuranech-huraveshvi

This posture is identical to that in Posture 10, except that the legs are reversed. The right heel is placed on top of the left knee.

These two postures release the 'scar tissue' of the psyche – the heart attachments and belief systems that form over lifetimes as a result of trauma.

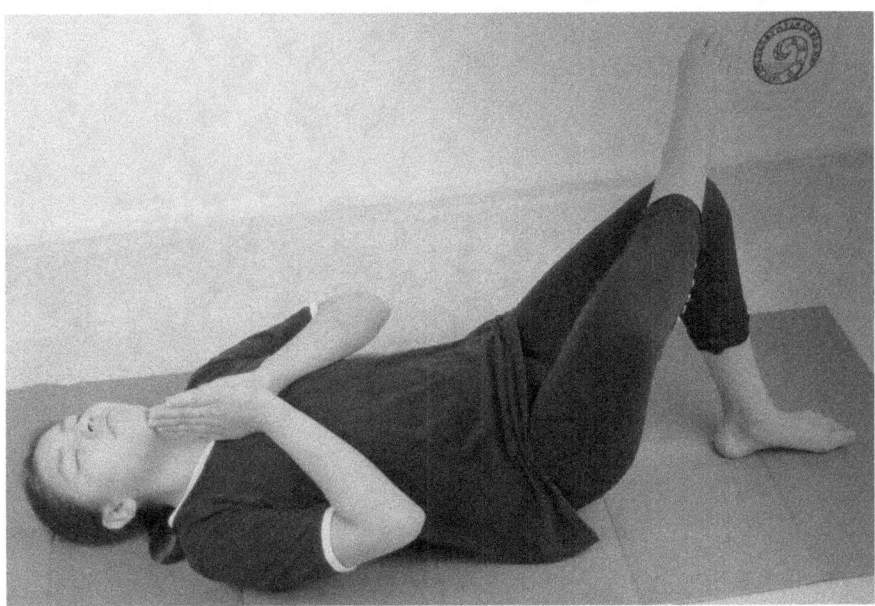

12. Posture No. 12 – Ubalech-spiruvat

- Lying flat on your back, bend your knees.
- Cross your feet and open your knees to the side as far as is comfortable, using pillows if necessary.
- Cross your arms and grasp the left earlobe with the right hand the right earlobe with the left hand.
- Rest your arms comfortably on your chest.

How to do the Yoga

- Maintain a steady pressure on the earlobes by holding them between the thumbs and forefingers.
- Breathe deeply as before.

Note: The pressure on the earlobes helps remove programmed reactions to external stimuli.

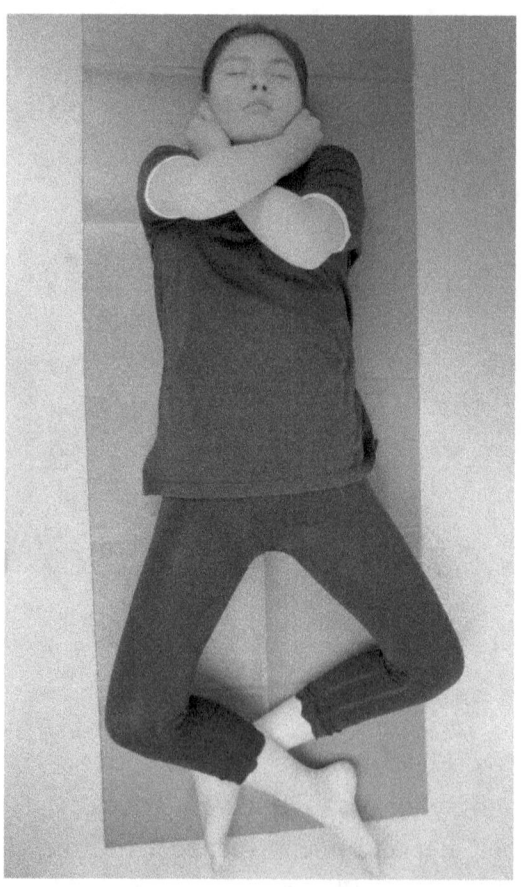

The 12 postures for the 12 most shallow or recent incarnation cycles are now complete.

The 12 Postures of the Oldest Incarnation Cycles

Kee-shahat aresbi minach verevaa skubivi. Kanech subetaa area paruhit. Kana su pirate eherevesbi surat.

Genius continually surpasses itself. Effortless knowing is its vehicle. Do not hold on to past standards.

THE 12 FEMININE POSTURES

Keesha arahes pa uhur nanu etaa.
Vires ese mista vu atres rubanes sutaa.

Reclaim now the gems that once were yours.
Release the dross that no longer serves.

13. Posture No. 13 – Sivaru-nanushtaa
- Sit in a cross-legged position with spine straight.
- With your hands extended in front of you and palms down, touch the tips of your index fingers and the tips of your thumbs together. The space between your hands will be diamond-shaped.
- Keeping your hands together as instructed, place them over the area of the pelvis where a woman's womb would be. The tips of the middle fingers would be right above the pubis bone.
- Roll your eyes upward and hold that eye position for the duration of this posture. The head stays facing forward.
- Breathe through the mouth in short, rapid staccato bursts[8]. The breaths are shallow and the area below the diaphragm and around the navel moves in and out with the bursts of breath.
- Like the lungs, the upper abdomen extends with in-breaths and deflates or contracts with out-breaths.
- The rhythm is rapid as in 'and one, and two and three' with the in-breaths happening on the 'and' and the out-breaths on the counts.

The breath is very important in this posture as it is designed to release eons of birth trauma.

---

[8] It will take practice to maintain this form of breathing throughout the sound elixir. Do not be discouraged if at first you cannot do it for the full duration.

How to do the Yoga

Posture No. 13

14. Posture No. 14 – Kirinat-subechva-anit

- Repeat everything as in Posture No. 13, but place the thumbs of the hand posture where the ribcage goes up in front in a V-shape. The diamond shape between the hands will rest over the solar plexus, the place where memories of insufficient mothering of the inner child are kept.
- Lie down if you get dizzy.

Separation angst is released through this posture

15. **Posture No. 15 – Keenan at-ukles-vivresbi**
   - Repeat everything given in Posture No. 13, <u>except that</u> –
   - The eyes will be looking downward as far as possible.
   - The hand position changes as follows:
   - Reach the hands behind you and with palms outward, place them over the sacrum in the lower back, the tips of the thumbs and index fingers together.
   - Again, there will be a diamond-shaped space between your hands but the palms will be facing outward. The index fingers will be on the coccyx bone. Separation angst is released through this posture.

16. Posture No. 16 – Kluset-miraveshta

The trauma of the past is held in the gap between breaths causing, in aggravated cases, stuttering, shortness of breath, sleep apnea and more. The technique of eliminating the gap between breaths can cause dizziness. Postures using this breathing technique are alternated with stretching postures to promote the removal of released toxins through increased lymph flow and to allow the participant to stabilize his or her breath. Take deep slow breaths so that you do not hyperventilate. Stop the breathing technique if you become dizzy.

- Lie flat on your back with your knees bent.
- Cross your forearms over each other and place them on your upper chest.
- Raise the hips off the floor, forming a straight line from the knees to the solar plexus. Use a pillow as support if needed.
- The eyes will look down on every in-breath. (The downward eye movement looks into unpleasant memories.)
- The eyes will look upward on the out-breath, releasing the unpleasant memories.
- While maintaining the posture, take long, deep breaths eliminating the gap between them as much as possible.

This posture targets the release of unpleasant physical memories.

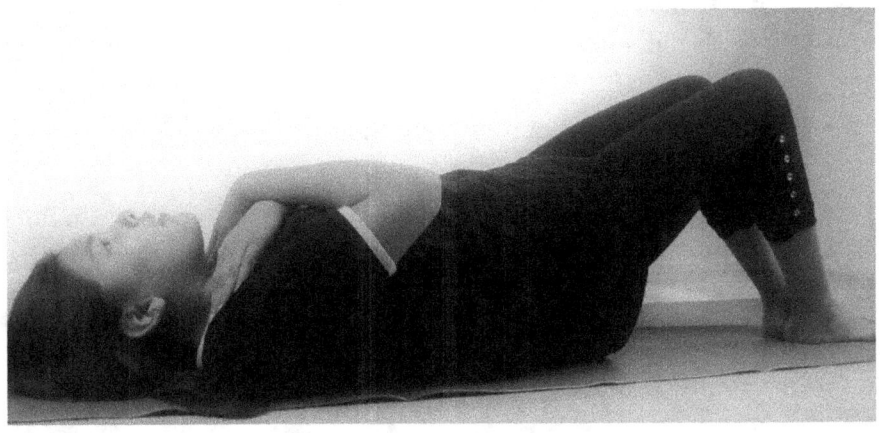

How to do the Yoga

17. **Posture No. 17 – Enatve-kluvesh**
    - While lying down, put your palms together over your heart, the bottoms of your feet together with your knees bent outward. Use two pillows to brace the knees if needed.
    - Relax the eyes and breathe normally. The body will be gently stretched but relaxed.

    The increased lymph flow promoted by this posture carries released toxins to excretion pathways.

18. **Posture No. 18 – Mishet-aranakvi-husat**
    - Sit with the soles of your feet together, knees bent and spine straight.
    - Cross the forearms across your chest.
    - Extend the index fingers.
    - Bend the remaining fingers and place the thumbs over them.
    - With the index fingers, push firmly on the areas inside the ears directly next to the ear opening.
    - With closed eyes, take deep breaths, eliminating the gaps between breaths.

- Maintain the pressure within the ears.

The subtle, subliminal memories accumulated as a result of debris held in the acupressure points of the body are targeted for release by this posture.

19. Posture No. 19 – Anak-bilashet

- In the same seated position as in Posture No. 18, reach your hands behind your head to the base of the skull (the medulla region).
- Cross the hands over each other in a V-shape with the fingers pointing slightly down.
- Breathe slowly and normally.
- Slowly move the eyes back and forth from side to side.
- Move the elbows out to the side until there is a comfortable stretch in the upper trapezius (shoulder) area.

The medulla is a significant storage area of memories from all lifetimes. This posture facilitates its clearing.

The 12 Postures of the Oldest Incarnation Cycles

20. Posture No. 20 – Mishet-arelu

The Arelu Postures in Nos. 20-24 (Arelu in the ancient language means 'little sun') are the culmination of the previous 19 postures. They do not entail eye movement or breath work, but use visualization to cleanse the spine, pranic tube and the fields around the body. They work as a progressive unit, cleansing the spinal cord and the neuro-pathways of the body, as well as the pranic tube and chakra system.

- Sitting with the soles of the feet together and spine straight, cup your hands together palms up (right hand on top) as though you were holding a ball the size of a large grapefruit.

How to do the Yoga

- Envision the ball as pale blue light and place it, within your cupped hands, at the top of your pubis bone.
- With every in-breath see the ball move up (your hands remain stationary) to the navel.
- With every out-breath move the ball back to the pubis.

21. **Posture No. 21 – Klavet-arelu**
    - Follow the same procedure as in Posture No. 20, but your cupped hands holding the ball of blue light are placed 2 inches below the navel.

The 12 Postures of the Oldest Incarnation Cycles

- With each in- and out-breath, the ball moves up and down between the navel and the heart.

22. **Posture No. 22 – Krivat-arelu**
    - Use the same procedures as in Postures No. 20 and 21, except this time the hands are cupped just below the heart.
    - With each in- and out-breath, the ball moves up and down between the heart and the throat (the bottom portion of the neck where swallowing takes place).

How to do the Yoga

23. **Posture No. 23 – Michpa-arelu**
    - Repeat the procedure in the previous three postures, but cup your hands at the bottom of your neck, elbows to the side.
    - With each breath, move the ball up and down between the throat and the top of the skull.
    - Envision the ball growing larger with each in-breath until it is the size of a large saucer.

24. Posture No. 24 – Paruk-nanastra-arelu

- Remain in the same seated position as in the preceding postures.
- Place the palms together and rest the hands on top of the head. Envision the ball of light the size of a large saucer resting on the tops of your fingertips.
- The ball remains stationary but grows larger and brighter during each in-breath until it reaches the size of a large dinner plate.[9]

---

9   As depicted in Egyptian and Sumerian art as a form of enlightenment.

How to do the Yoga

- At the end of the 24th sound elixir, take a deep breath and expel it through the mouth.
- Envision the ball above your head exploding on the forced out-breath and becoming large enough to enclose your whole body (even if you should stand). Because you are seated, it will extend into the floor beneath you.
- Remain in a relaxed state, moving your hands with palms up to rest on your knees (left hand on left knee, etc.).

Closing

The great significance of receiving the three bodies of yoga known collectively as Devi Satva Yoga, the Yoga of Illumination, is given in the ancient Scroll of Namud.

> *"For when once more eyes that can see*
> *Know the Yoga of Saradesi*
> *The third it shall be of three*
> *An end shall come to duality"*

The advent of the restoration of the three yogas to humanity heralds the onset of the next evolutionary state of human consciousness; Immortality through living a life of no opposites. How long it will take to achieve this is impossible to say when time does not in reality exist. But the fact that we have the tools to begin man's journey out of the Dream of Duality is cause for hope and gratitude.

With deep love I dedicate this information to the light bearers of the planet.

—Almine

ALMINE RECEIVES A SCROLL TO TRANSLATE

(As seen in inter-dimensional photography)

Taken in Sedona, Arizona Jan. 2010 while Almine was teaching. Note the scroll on her head.

Epilogue

The cleansing that takes place during the Arelu postures necessarily involves the chakras. For the convenience of the student, we provide an overview of the chakra system.

Chakras are energy vortices that act as interfaces between the levels of light in the cosmos and the physical. Light is received by the chakras acting as storage units or capacitors. They then download it to the physical component designed to receive light at a rate able to be received. The main physical components within the human body are the endocrine glands. However, reach cell is also equipped with its own miniscule chakra system.

As trauma or forced change (pain) occurs there is often a delay in processing the insights the experience yields. The accumulation of these suppressed insights creates a blockage or plug in the center of the chakra. Most people therefore have chakras that are conical to the front and back.

As we start living self-examined lives and extract the insights from past experience the chakras release their seals and become spherical. Eventually there is one large unified chakra field. Heartache, sexual stimulation, expanded awareness and other feelings usually localized within the area of a chakra now are felt in the entire body.

When the chakra fields unify a lot more energy is available to the individual and inner guidance becomes strong. The reason for this is that obstruction from the mental body is partially reduced and the influence of the higher bodies floods into the lower bodies. One begins to live in grace, to cooperate with the higher self in living the blueprint for this particular life.

Just prior to entry into God-consciousness a most miraculous experience transfigures the chakra field yet again. The symbol for this event was depicted by the ancients as a dove, beak pointed upwards, wings extended in a sphere or circle. This signifies the opening of five additional chakras utilized by someone in the second (God-conscious) and third (Immortal Mastery) stages.

The additional five chakras open as a result of incorporating all seven supporting attitudes into our lives. Their opening happens in a matter of minutes, unlike the more gradual opening of the other seven. This event may be preceded by physical discomfort and some bruising that comes and goes over major acupuncture points like the wrists.

The experience itself, however, is blissful and expansive. White light surrounded the body and a violet flame is visible on the head (like the description in the Bible of the Pentacostal flames). The light has a particular configuration resembling a dove with a circle above its head.

The opening occurs as follows:
1. The areas of the body where a woman's ovaries would be located burst open with white light; first the left and then immediately the right as chakras eight and nine open.
2. A skirt of light radiates downward, resembling the tail of the dove.
3. This ignites the pranic tube and a great rush of energy travels up from the base of the spine to the crown of the head and the violet flame appears.
4. Immediately afterwards a sphere of light about the size of a dinner plate appears about 8" above the head. It looks like the Sumerian and Egyptian art depicting the spheres above the heads of those with spiritual power. The tenth chakra is now open.
5. The eleventh chakra in the middle of the right shoulder blade and the twelfth chakra in the middle of the left shoulder blade open next and shoot out wings of light. Angelic beings who

have all twelve chakras open have been portrayed as having wings by those who can see energy directly.

6. The entire configuration of light at this point appears like a dove with a sphere above its head. There is a hidden reason why the ancients had the dove enclosed by a circle. The secret lies in the name the Lemurians gave to the number ten (remember the circle or sphere above the head is the tenth chakra). The number ten is called 'lahun' in Lemurian and some other ancient languages. "La" means all and 'hun' means one (la is 'all' backwards and languages still have words like 'un' or 'uno' that mean one).

The number ten means all in one and one in all (the Atlanteans also knew these secrets behind the law of the one). The sphere above the head will become larger and larger as we progress into the later stages of God-consciousness. At first it will extend all the way to the head, cleaving the flame into two 'horns' on either side (also depicted in ancient art). Eventually, when the Immortal Master overcomes all mortal boundaries, the sphere will enclose all other chakras. All is in one and one is in all.

Such a master now has the vehicle to travel at will with the speed of thought between dimensions and through space and time. The dove is now in the circle. The epitome of what a human being can be has been achieved.

Appendix I

NOTES FOR TEACHERS

The yoga may be taught to others if the practitioner has become proficient in its practices. No other training is needed because its effectiveness is inherent in its components.

Important Copyright Notice

This written material may be reprinted and taught as long as Almine is credited as its originator. The sound elixirs may be used to instruct others and may be reproduced for personal use only. They may not be distributed for sale or otherwise. They may be purchased from www.spiritualjourneys.com.

Appendix II

LIABILITY DISCLAIMER

Any liability, loss, damage or injury in connection with the use of this yoga and its instruction, including but not limited to any performance of the yoga, is expressly disclaimed by Spiritual Journeys, LLC and/or Almine.

Many have subluxations and misalignments in the neck. Seeking chiropractic treatment prior to attempting Shrihat Satva Yoga is beneficial. The next extensions and movements of Shrihat Satva Yoga should be done gently and with care not to strain the neck.

Yoga is not intended to diagnose illness or to constitute medical advice or treatment. Any student whose medical condition, including pregnancy or any other health-related condition that may affect performance of the yoga, is advised to consult with a physician or other qualified health provider prior to the start of this program and obtain approval to participate in the yoga.

OTHER BOOKS BY ALMINE

Irash Satva Yoga
The human body is unique in that it is an exact microcosm of the macrocosm of created life. There are 12 points along the right, masculine side of the body and the same number on the left side. These are microcosmic replicas of the macrocosmic cycles of life.

The yoga postures are designed to open and remove the debris from these points – the gates of dreaming. This will occur physically through the postures and the music. Dissolving debris also occurs by way of dreaming (triggered by the breathing and eye movements), releasing past issues that caused the blockages in the points.

Published: 2010, 108 pages, soft cover, 6 x 9, $24.95
ISBN: 978-1-934070-95-6

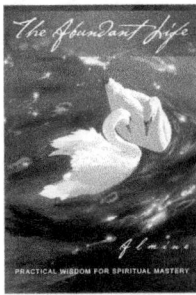

The Abundant Life
By popular demand, the profound words of wisdom that have changed the lives of more than 20,000 daily Twitter followers, communicating in multiple languages, have been compiled into book form.

Three hundred aphorisms and mandalas from the Seer Almine will delight and inspire her growing global audience.

Published: 2010, 188 pages, soft cover, 6 x 9, $19.95
ISBN: 978-1-934070-20-8

Almine is the author of many other books. All are available on http://www.spiritualjourneys.com

www.ingramcontent.com/pod-product-compliance
Lightning Source LLC
Chambersburg PA
CBHW070735230426
43665CB00016B/2252